To Wendi,
My sister, best friend, and hero.
I love you, sister of mine.
-Cheryl

This book is given with love

To:

_____

From:

_____

Dear Reader,

Feathers, just like birds, come in all shapes, sizes, and colors. Some feathers help a bird stay warm on a cold winter day while other feathers help a bird fly from tree-to-tree and even thousands of miles. Did you know that another name for feathers is "plumes"?

There is a name for people who study bird feathers; they're called "Plumologists".

Let's go on an adventure and learn a little more about birds and their amazing feathers, like how feathers are different colors, why some birds have waterproof feathers and some don't, and how birds keep their feathers clean and in tip-top shape.

- Cheryl Johnson

Learn More About Birds With...

Merlin Phone App:

Identify a bird with a photo, or if you don't have a photo, it will ask you 5 simple questions to help you figure out what the bird is.

Websites:

www.AllAboutBirds.org

www.ebird.org

www.FeederWatch.org

The Different Types of Feathers

A bird's feathers fit into six different groups
that all have their own unique and special purpose.

- Contour Feathers – cover most of the bird and include the wing and tail feathers
- Down Feathers – help keep a bird warm or cool
- Powder Down – help keep a bird's feathers waterproof
- Semiplumes – are for insulation and courtship
- Bristles – are tiny feathers found around a bird's mouth and eyes and help it catch food
- Filoplumes – are small, hairlike feathers about 1cm long and help a bird keep their flight feathers working well

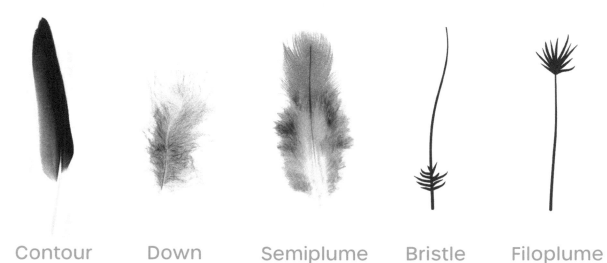

Contour   Down   Semiplume   Bristle   Filoplume

Fun Fact About Dinosaur Feathers

The feathers that dinosaurs had looked a lot different than the feathers of modern birds. Both dinosaur and bird feathers are made from keratin (which is also what scales are made of), but dinosaur feathers were very simple and looked more like long strands of hair rather than the feathers we know today.

Wood Storks

Modern Day Dinosaurs

Did you know that dinosaurs still walk among us? That's right, birds are descendants of the dinosaurs. Dinosaurs are the only ancient creatures that had feathers, and birds are the only modern day creatures that have feathers.

Unlike birds, most dinosaurs did not use their feathers to fly. Scientists believe dinosaurs used their feathers mostly to help them stay warm and attract a mate. Modern birds have changed a lot from their dinosaur ancestors, but when you look at some birds, like these Wood Storks, it's not hard to imagine what dinosaurs might have looked like with feathers!

Location & Season	Height	Weight	Habitat
Spring/Summer	Vacuum (40 Inches)	2 Toasters (4 Pounds)	Wetlands

Fall/Winter
Spent in South America

Fun Fact About Dimorphism

One of the main reasons that male birds have brighter colored feathers or more extravagant plumage than female birds is to help them attract a mate. Sometimes the males will combine their brightly colored feathers with a dance or a special song. This helps them stand out from the other males.

Summer Tanager

Same Bird, Different Plumage

Sometimes male and female birds of the same species look so much alike that it's hard to tell them apart, and sometimes, they can look like they are two completely different birds. For example, these two birds are both Summer Tanagers.

The male is bright red, and the female is a dull gold. When a male and female look completely different, it's called "dimorphism". Males usually have brighter colored feathers to help them attract a mate, and females usually have duller coloring to help them blend in to their surroundings and keep them safe from predators while they are raising their babies.

Location & Season	Height	Weight	Habitat
Spring/Summer	Dollar Bill (6 Inches)	2 Pencils (0.4 Ounces)	Woods

Fall/Winter
Spent in South America

Fun Fact About Egret Plumage

The feathers and breeding plumage of many birds, such as the Great Egret, became popular in women's fashions during the early 1900s. It was so popular that many of these birds were hunted almost to the point of extinction. Laws have since been passed to protect these and many other birds.

Great Egret

Breeding Plumage

One of the ways that birds use their feathers is to attract a mate. Each spring, the feathers on the males of many species will become brighter and prettier. Some birds will grow extra feathers like the Great Egret.

Each spring, both the male and female Great Egrets grow beautiful, extra tail feathers that they will fan out and display as the try to get the attention of the other Great Egrets. Often the birds with the longest feathers and brightest coloring are the most successful in getting a mate. These extra feathers and bright color changes are referred to as a bird's "breeding plumage".

Location & Season		Height	Weight	Habitat
Spring/Summer	Fall/Winter	Floor Lamp *(38 Inches)*	3 Soup Cans *(1.5 Pounds)*	Marsh

Fun Fact About Baby Bird Feathers

For many bird species, baby birds look more like their mother than their father, and this is to help keep them safe! Female birds, and baby birds alike, often have duller feather colors compared to adult males to help them blend in with their surroundings and keep them hidden from predators.

Indigo Bunting

Like Mama, Like Baby

This cute little Indigo Bunting isn't having a bad hair day; he's a young male that hasn't grown into his adult plumage yet. Many birds are born almost completely bald while others are born with soft feathers called "down", and many look completely different than their parents.

In the case of these Indigo Buntings, the first set of feathers they get are a dull brown color that helps them to blend into their surroundings. As Indigo Buntings grow, the females stay brown and the males get their bright blue feathers. It might take a male a few years for all of this "grown up" feathers to grow in.

Location & Season
Spring/Summer

Fall/Winter
Spent in South America

Height
Mobile Phone
(5 Inches)

Weight
Pencil
(0.2 Ounces)

Habitat
Woods

Fun Fact About Feather Colors

In many bird species, the male and female look so much alike that it's hard to tell them apart. Male and female Chickadees, Blue Jays, and Titmice look the same, but scientists believe that because birds can see more colors than humans, to them, the male and female feather colors can look completely different!

Painted Bunting

All The Colors Of The Rainbow

Bird feathers come in all the colors of the rainbow and some colors that we can't even see! That's because birds are able to see more colors than you or I can. In fact, birds have 25% more color receptors than people do, which allows them to see more colors.

You and I can only see what scientists call "natural light", but birds are also able to see UV or "ultraviolet light" allowing them to see colors that we literally can't even imagine. So, when you see a bird that looks dull and bland in color, that same bird might be as bright and beautiful to other birds as this Painted Bunting is to us.

Location & Season	Height	Weight	Habitat
Spring/Summer	**Light Bulb** *(5 Inches)*	**3 Quarters** *(0.6 Ounces)*	**Woods**

Fall/Winter
Spent in South America

Fun Fact About Feather Pigments

Some colors (or pigments), like brown, black, and gray are produced naturally by birds. It is called "melanin". Colors that appear in feathers like red, yellow, orange, and pink, come from foods with "carotenoids". Birds can make melanin in their bodies but can only get carotenoids from what they eat.

Roseate Spoonbill

You Are What You Eat

Have you ever been told "You are what you eat?" When it comes to the colors of some bird feathers, it's true! For example, Roseate Spoonbills and Flamingos get the pink color in their feathers from the food they eat, in this case, shrimp.

When Roseate Spoonbills are young, their feathers are light grey, but as they get older and gobble up all those yummy shrimps, their feathers turn pink. Carrots contain the same pigment (carotenoid) that are in shrimp. But don't worry, you'd have to eat lots of shrimp or carrots everyday for every meal before you would turn pink or orange!

Location & Season		Height	Weight	Habitat
Spring/Summer	Fall/Winter	Stool (30 Inches)	2 Basketballs (44 Ounces)	Marsh

Fun Fact About Green Feathers

Green is another color that isn't actually there. Do you know what color you get when you mix yellow and blue? Green! Green feathers happen when those microscopic air bubbles reflect blue light back through a yellow feather. A yellow feather mixed with blue light equals a feather that looks green to you and me.

Woodhouse's Scrub-Jay

When Blue Isn't Really Blue

When it comes to the color of bird feathers, would you believe that there is no such pigment color as blue? In reality, the actual color of a bird's blue feathers is gray. The blue color is created by tiny air bubbles in the feathers that are too small for you to see without a microscope.

When light hits these feathers, the air bubbles reflect the blue frequency light back off the feathers making them look blue. If you ever find a blue feather, hold it up so that the light shines through it and you'll see that the feather's color changes from blue to gray!

Location & Season	Height	Weight	Habitat
Spring/Summer	Tablet *(11 Inches)*	Deck of Cards *(3.4 Ounces)*	Woods

Fall/Winter
Spent in South America

Fun Fact About Crests

Some birds have crests that are almost always completely hidden.
Kinglets and Great Kiskadees have brightly colored feathers that are hidden
on the top of their head. When trying to show other birds who's boss,
these crests will pop up, and it will look like the top of their head is exploding!

Greater Roadrunner

Let Me Show You What's On My Mind

Many birds use their feathers to communicate with other birds. For example, a baby bird will flap its wings to tell its mom and dad that it's hungry. Some birds have feathers that form crests on the top of their heads that they use to let other birds know what it's thinking.

Often, these feathers will lay flat on the bird's head or are hidden from view completely, but when the bird is worried, curious, or is trying to "say" something to another bird such as, "I'm stronger and bigger so stay away" or "Hey, look at me. I'd make a good mate!" the crest will pop up.

Location & Season	Height	Weight	Habitat
Year Round	**Mirror** *(20 Inches)*	**Football** *(14 Ounces)*	**Woods**

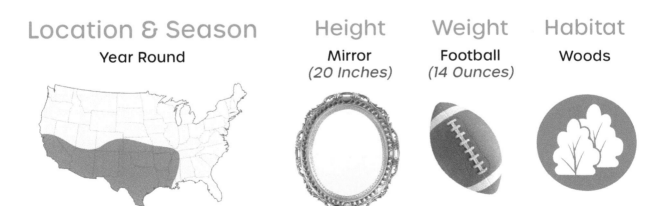

Fun Fact About Bristle Feathers

If you look closely at the face of this little bird, you'll see some feathers sticking out on either side of his beak, these are called "bristles". Bristles are often found on birds that catch insects while flying. Scientists think bristles help the bird to catch insects or even help the bird keep track of which way the wind is blowing.

American Redstart

Who Needs A Fork When You Have Feathers?

Some birds use their feathers to help them catch their dinner. This little warbler is a male American Redstart. He's a fast moving bird that never seems to sit still for very long. He eats insects, and as he hops around the branches of a tree or bush he will quickly flick his tail feathers up and down and opened and closed.

Scientists believe that he does this to startle insects and scare them out of their hiding places in the trees and under leaves. Once the insects have left their hiding places, the American Redstart will swoop after them, catch them, and gobble them up while flying.

Location & Season	Height	Weight	Habitat
Spring/Summer	Mobile Phone *(5 Inches)*	Quarter *(5.670 Grams)*	Forest

Fall/Winter
Spent in South America

Fun Fact About Feathers

Do you know what bird scientists think has the most feathers?
The Emperor Penguin! This large bird lives in the Arctic where it gets very cold,
and these penguins hunt for food by diving into the ocean. Their 80,000
feathers keep them warm and protected from the harsh climate.

Lark Sparrow

My, That's A Lot of Feathers

Have you ever wondered how many feathers a bird has? Turns out, they have quite a lot! Not surprisingly the smaller the bird, the fewer feathers it has. A hummingbird, one of the smallest birds on the planet, has only 1,000 feathers. Songbirds, like this Lark Sparrow, and other small birds you'll find fluttering around the trees have between 1,500 and 3,000 feathers.

Birds of prey, like hawks, have about 5,000 to 8,000 feathers and owls have about 20,000. Bigger birds like the Tundra Swan have about 25,000 feathers with 20,000 of those feathers covering the swan's long neck!

Location & Season		Height	Weight	Habitat
Spring/Summer	Fall/Winter	Light bulb (5 Inches)	2 Pencils (0.4 Ounces)	Grasslands

Fun Fact About Plucking

Most birds will lose feathers as they are preening, but some birds, like the Elder Duck, will pull feathers out of their body on purpose. They use the soft, downy feathers to make a nest for their babies. Keeping them warm and dry as they grow. When a bird pulls a feather out of its body, it's called "plucking".

Glossy Ibis

Keeping Those Feathers Neat and Tidy

As you've discovered, a bird's feathers are very important to its health and well-being for just about every aspect of its life. And if you've ever watched birds, you're bound to have seen one using its bill and its head to clean and organize his feathers. This is called "preening".

When a bird preens, it's not only removing dirt, bugs, and other things that might damage its feathers, it's also arranging, straightening, fixing, and waterproofing its feathers to make sure that they are in the best condition to help keep it warm, dry, and flying its best.

Location & Season	Height	Weight	Habitat
Year Round	Nightstand *(24 Inches)*	Basketball *(22 Ounces)*	Wetlands

Fun Fact About Waterproof Feathers

Some birds, like owls and pigeons, don't have a way of waterproofing their feathers, but instead, they have special feathers called "powder down". These feathers disintegrate into a fine, dust-like powder that coats the birds' other feathers, making them waterproof.

If Birds Are Waterproof Can They Float on Water?

Theoretically, most birds have waterproof feathers so they can float on water, but most birds cannot swim like ducks. Waterproofing is a very important feature for bird feathers as it helps birds to stay warm and dry, especially on cold and wet days.

A bird's feathers aren't naturally waterproof. Most birds have a special gland near their tail called a "preen gland" that produces a special waxy oil. When a bird is "preening", or cleaning its feathers, it'll rub its head over that gland and then rub its head over the rest of its feathers, using the oil to coat its feathers, making them waterproof.

Location & Season		Height	Weight	Habitat
Spring/Summer	Fall/Winter	Mirror *(20 Inches)*	2 Basketballs *(44 Ounces)*	Pond

Fun Facts About Dirt and Sunbathing

If water isn't handy, a bird will take a "dirt bath". That's right, it will sit in a pile of dirt and "splash" around just like it was in a puddle of water, using the dust to help clean its feathers. You might see a bird laying on the ground with its wings spread out. It's using the sun to help clean its feathers!

Yellow-Breasted Chat

If Feathers Are Waterproof, Why Do Birds Take Baths?

As we've learned, most birds have feathers that are waterproof. If that's the case, why do birds take baths? The truth is, scientists are not completely sure, but anyone who has a birdbath in their backyard knows birds take their bathtime very seriously!

Ornithologists (people who study birds) feel that birds bathe to help them keep their feathers clean, free of bugs that can damage their feathers, and to keep their feathers in good condition and tip-top shape. There is also some evidence that clean feathers help the bird to fly faster and more accurately.

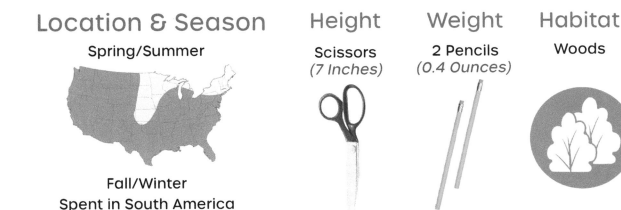

Location & Season	Height	Weight	Habitat
Spring/Summer	Scissors (7 Inches)	2 Pencils (0.4 Ounces)	Woods

Fall/Winter
Spent in South America

Fun Fact About Anhingas

Anhingas are also known as "Snake Birds", and if you've ever seen one looking for fish, you'll know why they have that name. Anhingas will slip into the water and swim around looking for fish, often with only their long, thin head and neck sticking out of the water which makes them look just like a snake!

Anhinga

Not All Birds Have Waterproof Feathers

Most birds have feathers that allow water to just slide right off, but some birds live on food they find in lakes and ponds such as fish, which means they have to swim under the water to catch their dinner. If they had waterproof feathers, it would make it harder for them to dive under the water to catch their meal.

These birds, like Anhingas, use their wet feathers to help them sink under the water and swim around looking for fish to gobble up. Since wet feathers make their bodies heavy, it's harder for them to fly, so they will perch with their wings spread out and use the sun to dry their wet feathers out before flying off.

Location & Season	Height	Weight	Habitat
Year Round	**Rocking Chair** *(32 inches)*	**2 Basketballs** *(44 Ounces)*	**Pond**

Fun Fact About How Birds Stay Warm

Most people have a body temperature of 98.6°F, but birds average about 105°F. On really cold nights, many smaller birds will snuggle together to help each other stay warm. Many birds grow extra feathers in the fall to give themselves extra warmth and protection in the winter.

Eastern Meadowlark

Built-In Insulation

Have you ever seen a bird sitting on a branch and its feathers are all fluffed out making it look like a little, round, puff ball? Chances are, it's a cold day and and the bird is using its feathers to help him stay warm.

The bird's "down" feathers help it stay warm on cold days, but when it needs a little extra warmth, it will fluff out its feathers and create pockets of air between its feathers and body, which gives it an extra layer of insulation and warmth. Sometimes, it'll even crouch low to tuck its legs into its feathers to help protect them from the cold too.

Location & Season	Height	Weight	Habitat
Year Round	Vase *(9 Inches)*	Baseball *(5 Ounces)*	Grasslands

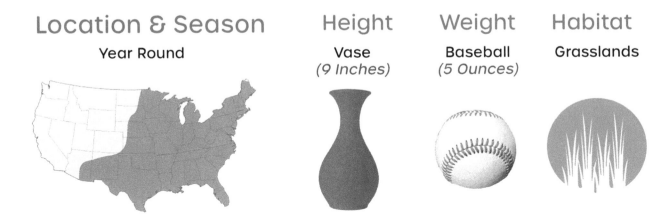

Fun Fact About Owl Feathers

When air travels over the wings of most birds as they fly, it disturbs the air and creates "turbulence" and air noise. Owl wings have a unique, serrated edge that looks like a comb. This edge helps the air flow quietly over the owl's wing so it can sneak up on its prey without being heard.

Great Horned Owl

Nature's Camouflage

For many birds, their feathers are an important part of the way they protect themselves from predators. Small birds, such as sparrows who live in trees and shrubs have brown colored feathers. These help them to blend in with the colors found in their habitat, making it hard for a predator, such as a hawk flying overhead, to see it.

Some birds have coloring that help them catch food. For example, owls hunt small birds and animals, and their feathers help them to hide in the trees and stay out of sight until a tasty meal wanders by, and then, they'll swoop down and catch it.

Location & Season	Height	Weight	Habitat
Year Round	Mirror (20 Inches)	3 Basketballs (66 Ounces)	Forest

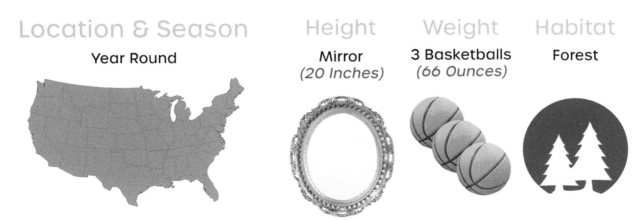

Fun Fact About Gathering Information on Birds

Did you notice that these birds have silver bracelets around their legs? This is known as "banding" and helps scientists learn more about birds such as how far they travel, how they move around or stay in the same place, and how long they live. Each band has a unique number issued by the Bird Banding Laboratory.

Northern Cardinal

Bald Really Is Beautiful!

Have you ever seen a bird sitting in the trees, and it just looks scruffy or is missing a whole bunch of feathers? Chances are, the bird is molting. "Molting" is when a bird loses its feathers and grows in new ones. It's a natural process and helps birds get rid of worn out feathers and grow in new ones.

Most birds molt once a year, usually in late summer. They will lose their old feathers in stages, and it can take a few weeks for their new feathers to completely grow in. So, if you see a bald bird like this Northern Cardinal, don't worry, chances are it's just molting.

Location & Season	Height	Weight	Habitat
Year Round	**Vase** *(9 Inches)*	**1 Golf Ball** *(1.620 Ounces)*	**Forest**

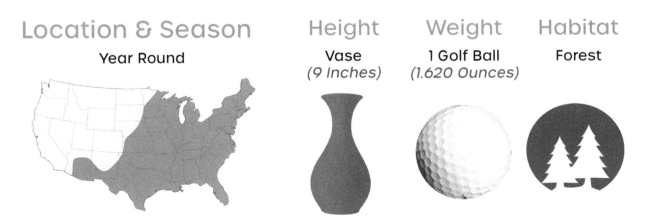

About the Author

Cheryl Johnson started on her "birding" journey in 2016. She has had a wonderful time learning about nature, discovering the incredible beauty that surrounds us, meeting lots of other fellow enthusiasts, and developing her skills and knowledge as a photographer and naturalist.

She stumbled upon wildlife photography by chance when she joined a bird walk through a local park as part of a magazine story she was writing and instantly fell in love with it! So, she grabbed her camera and prepared to take some "award-winning" photos of our fine, feathered friends because, really, how difficult could photographing birds really be? She soon discovered the answer: incredibly difficult! Not to be bested by the tiny, feathered creatures, she decided to figure out how it was done, and an obsession was born!

Cheryl started by purchasing feeders and photographing the birds visiting her backyard and soon found herself wandering all over town, up and down beaches, through forests, and all over the state snapping pictures of everything that flew past her lens.

Cheryl's award-winning photography has been featured in several publications, marketing campaigns, and websites. Her art has been displayed in several businesses: The Five Points Museum of Contemporary Art, and the Victoria Art League in Victoria, Texas. She's also been a guest speaker sharing her passion with many groups and organizations. When not traveling all over the state, country, and world photographing birds and other wildlife, she lives in Victoria, Texas, with her husband, two daughters, and her dog.

See Cheryl's Other Books:

"My Backyard Bird Book"

"My Book of Amazing Birds"

"My Bird Scavenger Hunt"

Visit Cheryl's Website:

www.CherylJohnsonAuthor.com

for more information
and photography

Junior Plumologist

Having completed the necessary course study, this is to certify that

 _____

is an official Junior Plumologist.

"May birds of a feather stick together!"

 # Claim Your FREE Gift!

Visit ➡ <u>PDICBooks.com/Gift</u>

Thank you for purchasing My Book of Plumology, and welcome to the Puppy Dogs & Ice Cream family.

We're certain you're going to love the little gift we've prepared for you at the website above.

Photograph Credit + Copyrights

CPSIA information can be obtained
at www.ICGtesting.com
Printed in the USA
BVHW021037070622
639118BV00007B/393